INVISIBLE DOG

Fabio Morábito was born to Italian parents in Alexandria in 1955 and has lived in Mexico City since the age of fifteen. He has published five collections of poetry, including *De lunes todo el año*, which won the Aguascalientes National Prize for Poetry in 1991 and *Lotes baldíos*, which was awarded the 1995 Carlos Pellicer prize. His poetry and short stories have established him as one of Mexico's best-known writers over the past thirty years. He has compiled and retold a book of 125 oral Mexican short stories, *Cuentos populares mexicanos* (2014), which won the 'White Raven Prize' in 2015. His novel *El lector a domicilio* (2018) was awarded the Xavier Villaurrutia Award. He is also a prolific translator from Italian, and his own books have been widely translated.

Richard Gwyn grew up in south Wales, and lived for many years in Greece and Spain. His travels in Latin America form the subject of a chronicle, *Ambassador of Nowhere* (2024). He is the author of four collections of poetry and three novels, and his memoir, *The Vagabond's Breakfast*, won Wales Book of the Year for nonfiction in 2012. He has translated poetry and short fiction by many Latin American writers. *The Other Tiger*, a major dual-text anthology of contemporary Latin American poetry, containing work by nearly 100 poets, was published by Seren in 2016. His translations of the poetry of Darío Jaramillo, *Impossible Loves* (Carcanet), was shortlisted for the Premio Valle-Inclán in 2020. His alter ego writes about literary and everyday matters on Ricardo Blanco's Blog.

Invisible Dog

FABIO MORÁBITO

translated by
RICHARD GWYN

CARCANET POETRY

First published in Great Britain in 2024 by
Carcanet
Alliance House, 30 Cross Street
Manchester, M2 7AQ
www.carcanet.co.uk

A CIP catalogue record for this book is
available from the British Library.

ISBN 978 1 80017 451 1

Book design by Andrew Latimer, Carcanet
Typesetting by LiteBook Prepress Services
Printed in Great Britain by SRP Ltd, Exeter, Devon

The publisher acknowledges financial
assistance from Arts Council England.

Contents

INVISIBLE DOG

IN LIMINE

Por el perdón del mar
nacen todas las playas
sin razón y sin orden,
una cada mil años
una cada cien mares.

Yo nací en una playa
de África, mis padres
me llevaron al norte,
a una ciudad febril,
hoy vivo en las montañas,

me acostumbré a la altura
y no escribo en mi lengua,
en ciertos días del año
me dan vértigos y mareos,
me vuelve la llanura,

parto hacia el mar que puedo,
llevo libros que no
leo, que nunca abrí,
los pájaros escriben
historias más sutiles.

Mi mar es este mar,
inerme, muy temprano,
cede a la tierra armas,
juguetes, sus manojos
de algas, sus veleidades,

from Lotes Baldíos (1985)

IN LIMINE

By the mercy of the sea
all beaches are born
for no reason and in no order,
one every thousand years,
one every hundred seas.

I was born on a beach
in Africa, my parents
took me north
to a hectic city,
today I live in the mountains.

I got used to the altitude
and I don't write in my language,
on certain days of the year
I suffer from fainting fits and vertigo,
the plain returns to me,

I leave for whatever sea I can,
I take books that I don't
read, that I never even opened,
the birds write
more subtle stories.

My sea is this sea,
defenceless, at first light,
it yields to the earth weapons,
toys, bunches
of algae, its whims,

emigra como un circo,
deja todo en barbecho:
la basura marina
que las mujeres aman
como una antigua hermana.

Por él que da la espalda
a todo, estoy de frente
a todo con mis ojos,
por él que pierde filo,
gano origen, terreno,

jadeo mi abecedario
variado y solitario
y encuentro al fin mi lengua
desértica de nómada,
mi suelo verdadero.

it migrates like a circus,
leaves everything fallow:
the sea's debris
that women love
like an older sister.

For the one who turns his back
on everything, I come
face to face with it all;
for the one who loses his edge,
I gain origins, land,

I gasp my varied and
solitary alphabet
and finally find my nomadic
desert tongue,
my true land.

SEIS LAGARTIJAS

I

¿Quién escribe en los muros?
¿Quién inventa los chistes?
¿Quién sella los refranes?

Es un puro regalo
que todos nos hacemos
esa escritura nómada,

anónima, interior,
que todos entendemos.
Una ciudad sin ella

no es nada, está bien muerta,
el exterior la come,
ya no se vive a sí,
ya no es capaz de un nombre.

II

La ciudad tiene lugares
donde no sucede nada,
lotes baldíos ocultos

tras una barda. Afuera,
un número de teléfono
se despinta, nadie compra.

SIX LIZARDS

I

Who writes on the walls?
Who invents the jokes?
Who provides the punchlines?

It's a perfect gift
we give ourselves,
this nomadic writing,

anonymous, interior,
something we all understand.
A city without it

is nothing, is properly dead,
the outside eats it,
it doesn't live for itself,
it doesn't even have a name.

II

The city has places
where nothing happens,
hidden vacant lots

behind an enclosing wall. Outside,
a painted telephone number
fades: no buyers.

Protegidos por el muro,
asciende la lagartija,
se espesa el matorral entre

basuras. Si hay otra vida,
que sea así. Atrás de un muro
ser sólo botellas rotas,
latas rendidas de lluvia.

III

Si esta ciudad tuviera
un río que dividiera
en dos a la ciudad

(un solo carnaval)
sería la prueba clara
de que existimos: unos

acá, otros allá.
Nos miraríamos
de frente – y otras veces

por dentro, cada uno,
al ver los remolinos,
la turbiedad del agua
debajo de los puentes.

IV

Si una noche las gentes
salieran a buscar
sus amigos de infancia

Protected by the wall,
the lizard climbs,
the scrub thickens between

piles of rubbish. If there's another life,
let it be like this. Broken bottles
behind a wall,
cans exhausted by the rain.

III

If this city had
a river that divided
it in two

(a single carnival)
it would be clear proof
that we exist: some

this side, others that.
We would look at ourselves
face on – and at other times

we'd look within, each of us,
on seeing the whirlpools,
the turbulence of the water
beneath the bridges.

IV

If one night people
went out to look for
their childhood friends

(¿no es eso un carnaval?)
los baldíos vivirían
su noche memorable.

¡La ciudad bajo llave
y la vida de nuevo
en torno a las fogatas,

en el nivel del suelo!
Un carnaval es sólo
esto: bajar, bajar,
bajar hasta el estruendo.

V

Que se cayó la barda,
la barda de madera
podrida del baldío.

Que se cayó por fin.
Selva y basura asoman
a la avenida intacta,

a la avenida música.
¿Qué dirán los periódicos,
los partidos, las cámaras?

Que me he caído a fondo,
amor, que ya me voy,
ya di de mí, ya sobro.
¿Qué dirán de nosotros?

(isn't that a carnival?)
the wastelands would have
a night to remember.

The city under lock and key
and life again
around the bonfires,

at ground level!
A carnival is just
that: going down and down
and down, into the uproar.

V

So the fence fell down,
the rotten wooden fence
around the vacant lot.

So it fell down, finally.
Weeds and rubbish spill out
onto the unsullied avenue

onto the musical avenue.
What will the papers say,
the political parties, the cameras?

So I've hit rock bottom,
love, and I'm leaving.
I've given it my all. Now I'm expendable.
What will they say about us?

VI

Bien. Ya tenemos muro;
hay que mirarlo, ahora,
imaginar la casa;

es el mejor momento
de una edificación:
todo es limpio y posible,

todo es un don del aire,
todavía no hay nada
que contar, sólo sueños.

Quedémonos un poco
en esta prehistoria,
esta tierra de nadie
donde el muro es de todos.

VI

Alright, we have a wall;
we'd best look at it, right now,
imagine the house;

it's the best moment
of the construction process:
everything is clean and possible,

everything is a gift of the air,
there is still nothing
to tell, only dreams.

Let's stay a little longer
in this prehistory,
this no man's land
where the wall belongs to everyone.

AJUSCO

Vaca, cuánta tristeza
en tus ojos ahora
que es lunes y el campo
es más inmenso y solo
y en torno a ti pululan
platos de cartón sucios
y latas de cerveza.

Pedazos de destierro
y calma se amontonan
en tu figura, vaca.
Miras alrededor
de ti, luego te agachas
hurgando en la basura
como un enorme perro.

Los restos de fogatas
parecen dentelladas
tuyas, no de los hombres
que incineran en ellas
antes de irse, último
rito de cohesión, vasos
de plástico y botellas.

La niebla cubre el cerro
y te rodea como
el mar a un promontorio,
y todo calla cuando
tu amplia maternidad,
de pronto, reclama entre
la bruma a tu becerro.

AJUSCO

Cow, how much sadness
in your eyes now
that it is Monday and the field
is more immense and lonely
and around you shimmer
dirty paper plates
and beer cans.

Slabs of exile
and calm accumulate
in your figure, cow.
You look around you,
then lower your head
to rummage in the trash
like an enormous dog.

The remains of campfires
resemble your tooth marks,
not those of the men
who, before leaving,
burned in them plastic cups
and bottles as a last
rite of cohesion.

The fog covers the hill
and encircles you like
the sea a promontory,
and everything is quiet when
your ample motherhood,
of a sudden, claims your calf
amid the mist.

BAHÍA QUINO

A Ethel

Esta mujer que abandona en la arena
su cuerpo es una roca que dibuja
la luz del mediodía, roca oscura
sin sed, sin ojos, sin sombra siquiera.

Esta mujer está tendida y sueña
que es una roca que la luz dibuja
en esta playa sin nombre. Sin duda
hay un ritmo de olas en sus venas.

En esta rada entra el mediodía
y borra los contornos de las rocas
y borra el mar de innumerables cuencas.

Y mientras sueña esta mujer tendida
que es una roca fija, una ola
se mete entre sus pies y la despierta.

BAHÍA QUINO

To Ethel

This woman, who abandons her body
to the sand, is a rock drawn by the midday light,
a dark and thirstless rock
without eyes, without even a shadow.

This woman is lying down and dreams
she is a rock drawn by the light
on this nameless beach. Doubtless
there is a rhythm of waves in her veins.

Into this inlet enters midday
erasing the contours of the rocks
erasing the countless sinkholes of the sea.

And while this woman lies dreaming
she's a solid rock, a wave
laps up between her feet, the wave that wakes her.

DESPEDIDA

Los martes
llegaba un mendigo
con mandolina
a la sombra del cidro
bajo nuestra ventana
de persianas verdes
que abría mi madre
para darle dos manzanas;
nos mudamos un día,
nos fuimos lejos,
el martes llegó el mendigo
a nuestra casa abandonada
y sé que estuvo
largo tiempo tocando
su mandolina
baja nuestra ventana
a la sombra del cidro
antes de irse para siempre
de la colina
de nuestra casa.

FAREWELL

On Tuesdays
a beggar used to come
with a mandolin
to the shade of the citron tree
beneath our window
with its green shutters
that my mother would open
to give him two apples;
one day we moved,
went far away,
on Tuesday the beggar came
to our abandoned house
and I know he was there
a long time playing
his mandolin
beneath our window
in the shade of the citron tree
before leaving for ever
the hill
where our house stood.

LA OLA QUE REGRESA

A Sandra Suter, que se quedó nadando

Si te revuelca la ola
procura que sea joven,
esbelta, ardiente,

te dejará molido el cuerpo
y el corazón más grande;

cuidate de las olas
retórica y viejas,
de las olas con prisa,

y la peor de todas,
de la ola asesina,

la ola que regresa.

THE RETURNING WAVE

To Sandra Suter, who kept on swimming

If the wave knocks you over
try to be young,
slender, ardent,

it will leave your body crushed
and your heart stronger;

beware of old and
rhetorical waves
of waves in a hurry,

and worst of all
the assassin wave,

the returning wave.

ÉPOCA DE CRISIS

Este edificio tiene
los ladrillos huecos,
se llega a saber todo
de los otros,
se aprende a distinguir
las voces y los coitos.
Unos aprenden a fingir
que son felices,
otros que son profundos.
A veces algún beso
de los pisos altos
se pierde en los departamentos
inferiores,
hay que bajar a recogerlo:
"Mi beso, por favor,
si es tan amable."
"Se lo guardé en papel periódico."
Un edificio tiene
su época de oro,
los años y el desgaste
lo adelgazan,
le dan un parecido
con la vida que transcurre.
La arquitectura pierde peso
y gana la costumbre,
gana el decoro.
La jerarquía de las paredes
se disuelve,

TIME OF CRISIS

This building
has hollow bricks,
you get to know everything
about the others,
learn to distinguish
between the voices and the lovemaking.
Some learn to pretend
that they are happy,
others that they are deep.
At times a kiss
from the upper floors
gets lost in the lower
apartments,
you have to go down and fetch it:
"My kiss please,
if you would be so kind."
"I kept it wrapped in a newspaper."
A building has
its golden age,
the years and fatigue
wear it thin,
so that it resembles
the life that passes by.
The architecture loses weight
and habit gains ground,
propriety gains ground.
The hierarchy of the walls
dissolves,

el techo, el piso, todo
se hace cóncavo,
es cuando huyen los jóvenes,
le dan vuelta al mundo.
Quieren vivir en edificios
vírgenes,
quieren por techo el techo
y por paredes las paredes,
no quieren otra índole
de espacio.
Este edificio no contenta
a nadie,
está en su época de crisis,
de derrumbarlo habría
que derrumbarlo ahora,
después va a ser difícil.

the roof, the floor, everything
turns concave,
this is when the young people flee,
travel the world.
They want to live
in virgin buildings,
they want a roof for a roof
and walls for walls,
they don't want
another kind of space.
This building doesn't satisfy
anyone,
it's in its time of crisis,
to knock it down you'd have
to knock it down right now,
later it's going to be difficult.

MUDANZA

A fuerza de mudarme
he aprendido a no pegar
los muebles a los muros,
a no clavar muy hondo,
a atornillar sólo lo justo.
He aprendido a respetar las huellas
de los viejos inquilinos:
un clavo, una moldura,
una pequeña ménsula,
que dejó en su lugar
aunque me estorben.
Algunas manchas las heredo
sin limpiarlas,
entro en la nueva casa
tratando de entender,
es más,
viendo por dónde habré de irme.
Dejo que la mudanza
se disuelva como una fiebre,
como una costra que se cae,
no quiero hacer ruido.
Porque los viejos inquilinos
nunca mueren.
Cuando nos vamos,
cuando dejamos otra vez
los muros como los tuvimos,
siempre queda algún clavo de ellos
en un rincón
o un estropicio
que no supimos resolver.

MOVING HOME

By moving home
I have learned not to glue
furniture to the walls,
not to hammer nails too deep,
only to turn the screw so far.
I have learned to respect the traces
of the old tenants:
a nail here, a moulding there,
a small bracket
left in its place,
even if these things bother me.
Some stains I inherit
without cleaning them,
I enter the new house
trying to understand,
or more like
seeing where I have to go.
I let the move
dissolve like a fever,
like a scab that falls off:
I don't want to make a din.
Because the old tenants
never die.
When we go on our way,
when we, in our turn, leave
the walls as we found them,
there will always remain some nail
of theirs, in a corner,
or something broken
that we didn't know how to fix.

AHORA, DESPUÉS DE CASI VEINTE AÑOS

A Mariapía Lamberti

Ahora,
después de casi veinte años
lo voy sintiendo:
como un músculo que se atrofia
por falta de ejercicio
o que ya tarda
en responder,
el italiano,
en que nací, lloré,
crecí dentro del mundo
—pero en el que no he amado
aún—,
se evade de mis manos,
ya no se adhiere
a las paredes como antes,
desierta de mis sueños
y de mis gestos,
se enfría,
se suelta a gajos.
Y yo,
que siempre vi ese vaso
lleno,
inextinguible,
plantado en mí
como un gran árbol,
como una segunda casa
en todas partes,
una certeza, un nudo
que nadie desataría
(un coto inaccesible,

NOW, AFTER ALMOST TWENTY YEARS

A Mariapía Lamberti

Now,
after almost twenty years,
I begin to feel it:
Just as a muscle atrophies
for want of exercise,
or takes its time
responding,
the Italian
in which I was born, wept,
grew up in the world
—but in which I have not yet
loved —
slips through my hands,
no longer sticks
to the walls like before,
deserts my dreams
and gestures,
becomes cold,
breaks away in segments.
And I,
who always saw that glass
as full,
inexhaustible,
planted within me
like a great tree,
like a second home
wherever I may be,
a certainty, a knot
that no one could untie
(an inaccessible preserve,

un refugio),
descubro una verdad
que por demás
siempre he sabido:
el que conquista
se descuida siempre
y por la espalda y la memoria
cojean los nómadas
y los advenedizos.
Hay que voltear atrás
tarde o temprano,
soldarse a algún pasado,
pagar todas las deudas
—de un sólo golpe
si es posible.
Así, si tú te vas,
idioma de mi lengua,
razón profunda
de mis torpezas
y de mis hallazgos,
¿con qué me quedo?,
¿con qué palabras
recordaré mi infancia,
con qué reconstruiré
el camino y sus enigmas?
¿Cómo completaré mi edad?

a refuge),
I discover a truth
that, as it happens,
I've always known:
the conqueror
is ever careless
and behind his back,
and in his memory,
nomads and upstarts limp on.
One has to turn back
sooner or later,
weld oneself to some notion of a past
pay one's debts
— all at once
if possible.
So, if you do leave,
language of my tongue,
hidden motive
behind my blunders
and my breakthroughs –
what remains for me?
With what words
will I recall my childhood,
with what will I reconstruct
the way and its wonders?
How will I complete the circle of my years?

LA LUNA LLENA

Después de recibir la carta
de mi padre, mi madre
comenzó a vender
los muebles,
quería costear el viaje
dejando intacto los ahorros.
Venían los compradores
y una señora se llevaba el radio
o la televisión, otra un tapete,
otra un florero.
La casa se vaciaba sin criterio.
Mi hermano y yo,
de vuelta a casa,
mirábamos la luna
que entraba a manos llenas en los cuartos.
Mi madre ya dormía, o casi.
Dejábamos las luces apagadas
por los moscos.
Quedaba poco: un clóset,
nuestras camas,
el refri y unas lámparas.
La vida así, sin nuestro padre
y sin los muebles,
era un paréntesis.
No daban ganas de dormirse.
Mi hermano se servía
su limonada y se sentaba
en uno de los dos balcones,
yo en el balcón de otro lado.
Mirábamos el mismo cielo.

FULL MOON

After receiving my father's
letter, my mother
began to sell
the furniture,
she wanted to pay for the journey
without touching her savings.
The buyers came
and one lady took away the radio
or the television, another a rug,
another a vase.
The house emptied out at random.
My brother and I,
back home again,
looked at the moon,
as it flooded the rooms.
My mother was sleeping by now, or nearly.
We switched off the lights
on account of the mosquitoes.
Not much remained: a wardrobe,
our beds,
the fridge and some lamps.
Life like that, without our father
and without the furniture
was a life between parentheses.
We didn't feel like sleeping.
My brother poured himself
a lemonade and sat
on one of the two balconies,
and I sat on the other.
We looked at the same sky.

Era como velar el sueño de mi madre,
como haber sido siempre adultos.
La luna entraba
y no encontraba
obstáculos.
Estábamos de vacaciones
hasta el vértigo, teníamos
entre manos
un viaje sin regreso.
Mi hermano hacía sonar
los hielos de su vaso,
yo no sabía hacer nada aún,
estaba íntegramente vivo,
íntegramente inexpresivo.
No sé si era feliz
o desdichado,
pero absorbí
ese verano que fue el último
como un resumen
de mi infancia,
como la cifra de una edad
cerrada de un portazo,
y en eso tuve suerte:
poder decir se terminó,
aquí se corta esta madeja,
reunir en un lugar
toda una época,
es enterrar de veras algo,
tener conciencia
de lo que es estar vivo,
antiguo como cualquier piedra.
Y si la veo
que sigue recorriendo el cielo

It was like watching over my mother's sleep,
as if we had always been adults.
The moon entered
and found
no obstacles.
We were on a vertiginous vacation,
we had between
our hands
a one-way ticket.
My brother rattled
the ice cubes in his glass,
I didn't know how to do anything yet,
I was utterly alive,
utterly blank.
I don't know if I was happy
or sad,
but I soaked up
that summer, which was the last,
like a recap
of my childhood,
like the cipher of an era
slammed shut,
and in that I was lucky:
it could be said it ended,
here the thread is cut,
to gather an entire epoch
in one place
is to truly bury something,
to be conscious
of what it is to be alive,
ancient as any rock.
And if I see
that she continues to cross

idéntica, invariable,
como diciendo soy la misma
y ustedes son los mismos,
todo es lo mismo para siempre
y el tiempo no dio un paso desde entonces,
ya no le creo, y si le creo,
ya no me turba como antes.

the identical, unchanging sky,
as though saying I am the same
and you are the same,
everything is the same forever
and time has not moved on since then,
I no longer believe her, and if I believe her,
it doesn't bother me like it used to.

UN VIAJE A PÁTZCUARO

A los dieciséis años,
sin un motivo claro,
compré un boleto para Pátzcuaro.
Viajé toda la noche en un camión
semivacío.
Pude haber ido
a Zacatecas o a Querétaro,
o a cualquier otra parte.
Nunca viajaba rumbo al mar,
el mar era la meta de los viejos,
quitaba a un viaje su heroísmo.
Llegué al amanecer
a Pátzcuaro,
la plaza estaba sola,
desiertos los portales,
sólo se oían mis pasos,
como en un cuadro de De Chirico.
Un primer rayo se posaba
en la cabeza de la estatua
de Quiroga.
Una mujer salió a barrer
la acera, la acera de un hotel
que a mí me pareció de lujo
(porque tenía dieciséis años),
y me ofreció una habitación.
Estaba en el segundo piso.
Daba a la estatua,
tenía un balcón,
tenía una mesa hermosa
junto a la ventana,
era muy amplia y luminosa.

JOURNEY TO PÁTZCUARO

At sixteen years of age
with no clear purpose in mind,
I bought a ticket for Pátzcuaro.
I travelled all night
in a half-empty bus.
I could have gone
to Zacatecas or to Querétaro,
or any other place.
I never travelled to the sea,
the sea was where old people went,
it detracted from the journey's heroism.
I arrived at Pátzcuaro
at dawn,
the square was empty,
the doorways deserted,
only my footsteps could be heard,
like in a painting by De Chirico.
The sun's first rays
lit up the head
of Quiroga's statue.
A woman came out to sweep
the pavement outside a hotel
that seemed to me luxurious
(because I was sixteen)
and offered me a room.
It was on the second floor.
It looked out over the statue,
it had a balcony,
and a fine table
next to the window,
it was spacious and well-lit.

No me atreví a tomarla.
Y ése era el cuarto
idóneo para mí,
tenía la luz
de mis dieciséis años.
Tal vez ahora sería otro,
todo sería distinto,
no escribiría lo que escribo.
¿Quién volverá a ofrecerme
en el silencio de una plaza
un cuarto así, enfrente de una estatua?
Tal vez no he vuelto a tener años
desde entonces,
soy todo lo que fui a los dieciséis
o un poco menos.
En otro hotel,
oscuro y anodino,
al que me fui a meter
a tres o cuatro cuadras de la plaza,
alguien gritó que me callara
cuando empecé a tocar guitarra.
No había balcón y la ventana
daba a un patio gris.
Cómo me odié despacio
por ese viaje
que no sabía llevar a cabo.
¿Por qué venir a Pátzcuaro, a Janitzio,
por qué cargar con la guitarra
si apenas la tocaba,
por qué tocarla, si así
sólo apuraba mi regreso
y todo me era indiferente?
¿Por qué viajar
para volver,

I didn't dare take it.
And that was the ideal
room for me,
it had the radiance
of my sixteen years.
Maybe now I would be someone else,
everything would be different,
I wouldn't write what I write.
Who would offer me
such a room again, overlooking a statue
in the silence of a square?
Maybe I haven't aged since then,
I'm everything I was at sixteen
or a little less.
In another hotel
dark and dull,
three or four blocks from the square,
in which I took a room,
someone yelled at me to shut up
when I began to play the guitar.
There was no balcony and the window
gave onto a grey patio.
Gradually I grew to hate myself
for not knowing how
to make that journey.
Why did I come to Pátzcuaro, to Janitzio,
why did I lug around the guitar
that I barely ever played,
why play it at all, if it
only hastened my return
and everything left me so indifferent?
Why travel
in order to return,
to test myself, with blinkered eyes?

para probarse, tapándose los ojos?
Estuve a un pelo de tener mi edad,
tal vez,
a un pelo de tocar el fondo sin dolor.
¡El viejo vicio de los míos
de creer en la experiencia,
no en los ojos,
y no coger al vuelo nada,
como un pecado!
No estuve cuatro días en Pátzcuaro,
sólo el primer minuto,
y sólo en ese tiempo fui perfecto,
el tiempo de dar vuelta a los portales
si nadie que me viera ni me oyera,
como en un cuadro de De Chirico.

I was within a hair's breadth
of acting my age,
perhaps,
within a hair's breadth of touching the depths
without pain.
The old vice of my kin
of believing in experience, not in my eyes,
and not grabbing anything on the fly,
as though it were a sin!
I wasn't four days in Pátzcuaro,
and only for the first minute,
only then was I perfect,
when I wandered past the doorways
and no one could see me, no one hear me,
like in a painting by De Chirico.

LOS COLUMPIOS

Los columpios no son noticia,
son simples como un hueso
o como un horizonte,
funcionan con un cuerpo
y su manutención estriba
en una mano de pintura
cada tanto,
cada generación los pinta
de un color distinto
(para realzar su infancia)
pero los deja como son,
no se investigan nuevas formas
de columpios,
no hay competencias de columpios,
no se dan clases de columpio,
nadie se roba los columpios,
la radio no transmite rechinidos
de columpios,
cada generación los pinta
de un color distinto
para acordarse de ellos,
ellos que inician a los niños
en los paréntesis,
en la melancolía,
en la inutilidad de los esfuerzos
para ser distintos,
donde los niños queman
sus reservas de imposible,
sus últimas metamorfosis,
hasta que un día, sin una gota

SWINGS

Swings are not news,
they are as simple as a bone
or a horizon,
they work with a body
and their upkeep requires
no more than a coat of paint
every once in a while,
though every generation paints them
in a different colour
(to enhance their childhood)
but otherwise leaves them
as they are.
No one investigates
new styles of swings,
there are no swing competitions,
no swing classes are delivered,
no one steals swings,
the radio doesn't transmit
the sound of creaking swings,
each generation paints them
in a different colour
to remind themselves
of the way that swings initiate children
at break time,
in melancholy,
in the futility of their efforts
to be different,
where children burn
their reserves of the impossible,
their latest metamorphoses,

de humedad, se bajan
del columpio
hacia sí mismos,
hacia su nombre propio
y verdadero, hacia
su muerte todavía lejana.

until on a day without a drop
of humidity, they get down
from the swing,
towards themselves,
towards their own true name,
towards their own still distant death.

SOLLOZOS

Yo siempre llego tarde
a los entierros,
cuando los ojos
de los concurrentes
se han secado
y algunos ya olvidaron
la cara del difunto,
qué edad tenía,
de qué murió.
Entonces llego yo
con mi llanto anacrónico,
con el negro de mi luto
en todo su candor aún,
reparto abrazos
como incendios,
retengo entre mis manos
las manos de la viuda
y de los huérfanos,
todo el cortejo asiste
a mi dolor,
nadie se atreve a contrariarlo,
la gente se avergüenza
y vuelve a apretujarse
alrededor del muerto,
la viuda no resiste
y rompe a sollozar,
los huérfanos también
y el llanto crece nuevamente,
alcanza a todos,
a los que no habían llorado aún,
a los que andan por ahí,

SOBBING

I always arrive late
at funerals,
when the eyes
of those attending
have dried
and some have already forgotten
the face of the deceased,
how old he was,
the cause of his death.
Then I arrive
with my anachronistic weeping,
in my honest mourner's black
and like a conflagration
I offer out hugs,
clasp the hands of the widow
and of the orphans
between my hands,
the whole cortège witnesses
my pain,
no one dares refute it,
people are embarrassed
and crowd together again
around the dead man,
the widow caves in
and breaks into sobs,
the orphans also
and the sound of weeping grows once more,
reaching everyone,
those who have not yet wept,
those who are there
who observe that it is the weeping

que advierten que es un llanto de reflujo,
de envergadura,
y entran en él,
se olvidan de sus muertos
o los recuerdan con más claridad,
y el llanto se hace caudaloso,
arrastra llantos de otras épocas,
se advierte su bramido de gran llanto
que se expande
y se desliga de los muertos,
por eso llego tarde
al llanto de los otros,
vengo con otro llanto
en la garganta
que suelto entre los cuerpos húmedos
y veo cómo se prende en cada lágrima,
se enrosca,
crepita en cada uno,
y soy el único que sabe
que es mu desdicha
la que están llorando,
que están llorando por mis muertos
y me regalan sus sollozos.

of a returning tide
of considerable magnitude,
and they enter into it,
they forget about their dead
or remember them with greater clarity,
and the weeping flows faster,
dragging with it the weeping of other occasions,
its roar warns of a great weeping
which broadens out
and detaches itself from the dead,
for this I arrive late
at the weeping of others,
I come with another weeping
in my throat
which I let loose among the damp bodies
and I see how it clings to every tear
coils around,
crackles in each of them,
and I am the only one who knows
it is my misfortune
they are weeping for,
that they are weeping for my dead
and bestow their weeping on me.

PARA QUE SE FUERA LA MOSCA

Para que se fuera la mosca
abrí los vidrios
y continué escribiendo.
Era una mosca chica,
no hacía ruido,
no me estorbaba en lo más mínimo,
pero tal vez empezaría
a zumbar.
Un aire frío,
suave,
entró en el cuarto;
no me estorbaba en lo más mínimo,
pero no se llevaba
con mis versos.
Cambié mis versos,
los hice menos melodiosos,
quité los puntos,
los materiales de sostén,
las costras adheridas.
Miré la mosca adolescente y gris,
sin experiencia;
no se movía del mismo punto,
tal vez
buscaba entrar en la corriente
de las moscas,
buscaba a su manera unas palabras mágicas.
Rompí mis versos,
a fuerza de quitarles costras
habían quedado ajenos.

TO LET OUT THE FLY

To let out the fly
I opened the window
and continued writing.
It was a small fly,
it didn't make a noise,
it didn't disturb me in the least,
but perhaps it would begin
to buzz.
Cold air,
gentle air
entered the room;
it didn't disturb me in the least,
but it didn't sit well
with my verses.
I changed my verses,
I made them less melodious,
I left out the full stops,
supporting materials,
the sticky encrustations.
I looked at the fly, young and grey,
inexperienced:
it didn't move from the same spot,
perhaps
it was looking to join the mob
of flies,
it was seeking, after its fashion,
some magic words.
I broke up my verses:
by removing the scabs,

Fui a la ventana,
por un momento
todo lo vi como una mosca,
el aire impracticable,
el mundo impracticable,
la espera de un resquicio,
de una blandura
y del valor
para atreverse.
Fuimos el mismo adolescente gris,
el mismo que no vuela.
¿Qué versos que calaran hondo
no venían,
de esos que nadie escribe,
que están escritos ya,
que inventan al poeta que los dice?
Porque los versos no se inventan,
los versos vienen y se forman
en el instante justo de quietud
que se consigue,
cuando se está a la escucha
como nunca.

they had become strange.
I went to the window,
for a moment
I saw everything as a fly does,
the impassable air,
the impassable world,
the hunt for a crack,
for a weakness
and for the courage
to dare.
We were the same grey teenager,
the one who doesn't fly.
What deeply-wrought verses
did not arrive,
those that nobody writes,
that are already written,
that invent the poet who speaks them?
Because verses are not invented,
verses come and are formed
at the precise moment of stillness
that is reached
when you are listening
like never before.

PUESTO QUE ESCRIBO

Puesto que escribo en una lengua
que aprendí,
tengo que despertar
cuando los otros duermen.
Escribo como quien recoge agua
de los muros,
me inspira el primer sol
de las paredes.
Despierto antes que todos,
pero en alto.
Escribo antes que amanezca,
cuando soy casi el único despierto
y puedo equivocarme
en una lengua que aprendí.
Verso tras verso
busco la prosa de este idioma
que no es mío.
No busco su poesía,
sino bajar del piso alto
en que amanezco.
Verso tras verso busco,
mientras los otros duermen,
adelantarme a la lección del día.
Oigo el ruido de la bomba
que sube el agua a los tinacos
y mientras sube el agua
y el edificio se humedece,
desconecto el otro idioma
que en el sueño
entró en mis sueños,
y mientras el agua sube,

BECAUSE I WRITE

Because I write in a language
that I learned,
I have to be awake
while others sleep.
I write like someone
scraping water from the walls,
and am inspired by
the early sun inside my room.
I wake before everyone,
but up above.
I write before daybreak,
when I am almost the only one awake,
and can make mistakes
in a language that I learned.
Line after line
I seek out the prose of this language
that is not mine.
I don't seek out its poetry,
but descend from the top floor
in which I wake.
I trawl through line after line
while others sleep,
stealing a march on the day's lesson.
I hear the sound of the pump
that draws water to the tanks
and as the water rises
the building becomes humid,
I disconnect the other language
which in sleep
enters my dreams
and while the water rises

desciendo verso a verso como quien
recoge idioma de los muros
y llego tan abajo a veces,
tan hermoso,
que puedo permitirme,
como un lujo,
algún recuerdo.

I descend line by line, like one
who recognises the language of the walls
and I reach so far down at times,
and it is so lovely
that I allow myself,
as a luxury
some small remembrance.

DESPIERTO CUANDO NO AMANECE AÚN

Despierto cuando no amanece aún,
prendo la luz de mi escritorio y miro
si es la primera luz del edificio.
En realidad casi no escribo,
vigilo cómo nace el día,
cómo se encienden otras luces
de otros predios.
Los días que mi escritura
no se enciende,
afuera nadie se amotina.
Las luces se arrodillan
cuando ya amanece.
La mía del escritorio se resiste,
pero claudica como todas.
La tinta, si ha fluido,
tiene una prueba que pasar.
Se lee con otros ojos
lo que dictó la oscuridad,
que es todavía luz de ayer.
Con luz de ayer se escribe,
a oscuras, para que amanezca.

I WAKE WHEN IT'S NOT YET DAWN

I wake when it's not yet dawn,
switch on my desk lamp and look
to see if it's the first light in the building.
As a matter of fact I barely write,
I watch how the day comes to life,
as other lights come on
in other properties.
On days when my writing
does not catch fire
nobody riots outside.
The lights bow down
when the dawn breaks.
Mine, on the desk, resists,
but gives in, like the rest of them.
The ink, if it has flowed,
has a test to pass.
One reads with different eyes
whatever was dictated by the darkness,
which is still yesterday's light.
With yesterday's light one writes,
in the dark, so that it might dawn.

YO VINE AL MUNDO

Yo vine al mundo
en la ciudad más prostituida,
más circular,
más envidiada,
todo se deteriora
al acercarse de ella,
todo trabaja en su favor
para dejarla inalcanzable.
A lo mejor se nace siempre así,
a lo mejor todos nacimos en Alejandria.
Jamás he de volver a verla
porque mi edad, mis versos
(¿no so los mismo?)
se han hecho
de esta lejanía,
no de otra cosa.
Mi verdadero lujo
es este: haber nacido
donde no he de volver jamás,
casi no haber nacido.
Cuando me muera,
si he de morir,
me moriré más lejos que ninguno.

I CAME INTO THE WORLD

I came into the world
in the most prostituted,
most circular,
most coveted city,
everything gets worse
on approaching her,
everything works in her favour
to keep her out of reach.
Perhaps it always starts out that way,
perhaps we were all born in Alexandria.
I never have to return to see her
because my age, my poems
(are they not the same?)
are made of
this distance,
and of nothing else.
My true luxury
is this: to have been born
where I never need to return
is almost not to have been born.
When I die
if I have to die,
I will die further away than anyone.

SÓLO HAY CANTO

Sólo hay canto
porque hay montañas,
porque lo que decimos
las montañas lo deforman,
y así se forma,
con las palabras desvirtuadas
por los montes,
como el deseo de oírse
por primera vez,
el canto.
Ellas nos enseñaron
a no tener del todo la razón,
a suspendernos
y esperar.
Cuando aprendimos a callarnos
pudimos aprender a oírlo todo
sin asustarnos más
de lo que oíamos,
y en las palabras
desvirtuadas por los montes
reconocimos un anhelo
que las palabras no decían.
Así, silencio y canto
vienen juntos
y para algunos son lo mismo,
porque después de los silencios
más profundos,
para volver a pronunciar
cualquier palabra,
es imposible no cantar.

THERE IS ONLY SONG

There is only song
because there are mountains,
because the things we say
are deformed by the mountains,
and thus,
with words distorted
by the hills,
– like the desire to be heard
for the first time –
the song.
They taught us
that we didn't have to be completely right,
and to be still
and wait.
When we learned to shut up
we learned to hear everything
without being scared
by what we heard,
and in the words distorted
by the mountains,
we recognised a longing
unspoken by the words.
So, silence and song
come together
and for some they are the same,
because after the deepest
silences,
to utter any word again
it is impossible not to sing.

EN EL PASILLO

En el pasillo,
mientras leo,
se abre una puerta y se cierra,
se abre y se cierra,
y yo espero que se acabe su agonía.
Dicen que cuando el aire
abre y cierra una puerta,
alguien muy cerca está en peligro.
Hay que prestar oído,
cerrar el libro que leíamos
y unirnos a ese rezo;
no levantarnos a cerrar la puerta,
sino quedarnos quietos y oír, oír
hasta sacarle alguna música al crujido.

IN THE CORRIDOR

In the corridor
while I read,
a door opens and shuts,
opens and shuts,
and I hope that its agony will end.
They say that when the draught
opens and shuts a door,
someone close to us is in danger.
We have to listen carefully,
close the book that we were reading
and join in that prayer;
not get up to shut the door,
but stay still and listen, listen
until the creaking turns to music.

UN PERRO INVISIBLE

Tengo un perro invisible,
llevo un cuadrúpedo por dentro
que saco al parque
como los otros a sus perros.
Los otros perros,
cuando al doblarme
lo dejo en libertad
para que juegue y corra, lo persiguen,
sólo sus dueños no lo ven,
tal vez tampoco a mí me vean.
Se ha ido dando a fuerza de paseos,
anima e inquieta a la perrada
y entre los dueños cunde la inquietud
y llaman a sus perros
para que no se forme la jauría.
Tal vez tampoco a mí me vean,
sentado en una banca,
doblado un poco
por el esfuerzo de dejarlo libre,
y aunque no pueden verlo,
tal vez sí ven al perro
que invisible, como el mío,
llevan dentro,
la bestia que no sacan nunca,
el perro que reprimen
llevando de paseo a sus perros.

INVISIBLE DOG

I have an invisible dog,
I carry a quadruped inside me
that I let out in the park
just as others do their dogs.
When I bend down
to let him go free,
to play and run,
the other dogs chase him,
only their owners don't see him,
maybe they don't see me either.
It happens more and more with every outing
the other dogs get worked up into a state
and among the owners a disquiet grows
and they call their dogs
to prevent a pack from forming.
Maybe they don't see me either,
sitting on a bench,
doubled over a little
with the effort of letting him go free,
and although they can't see him,
perhaps they do see the dog
they carry inside,
invisible like my own,
the beast they never release,
the dog that they repress
while taking their dogs for a walk.

NO HE AMADO

No he amado bastante
las sillas.
Les he dado siempre
la espalda
y apenas las distingo
o las recuerdo.
Limpio las de mi casa
sin fijarme
y solo con esfuerzo puedo
vislumbrar
algunas sillas de mi infancia,
normales sillas de madera
que estaban en la sala
y, cuando se renovó la sala,
fueron a dar a la cocina.
Normales sillas de madera,
aunque jamás
se llega a lo más simple
de una silla,
se puede empobrecer
la silla más modesta,
quitar siempre un ángulo,
una curva,
nunca se llega al arquetipo
de la silla.
No he amado bastante
casi nada,
para enterarme necesito
un trato asiduo,
nunca recojo nada al vuelo,
dejo pasar la encrespadura

I HAVEN'T LOVED

I haven't loved chairs enough.
I've always turned
my back on them
and can hardly tell
one from the other
or remember them.
I clean those in my house
without paying attention
and only with an effort can I
bring to mind
certain chairs of my childhood,
ordinary wooden chairs
that were in the dining room
and which, when the dining room was renovated,
furnished the kitchen.
Ordinary wooden chairs,
although you never arrive at
the true simplicity
of a chair,
you can impoverish
the most modest chair,
always remove an angle,
a curve,
you never get to the archetype
of the chair.
I haven't loved
almost anything enough,
to notice what is really there
requires an assiduous connection,
I never pick up anything on the fly,
I let the friction of the moment

del momento, me retiro,
solo si me sumerjo en algo existo
y a veces ya es inútil,
se ha ido la verdad al fondo
más prosaico.
He amortiguado demasiadas
cosas para verlas,
he amortiguado el brillo
creyéndolo un ornato,
y cuando me he dejado seducir
por lo más simple,
mi amor a la profundidad
me ha entorpecido.

pass, I withdraw,
only when I immerse myself in something do I exist
and at times it's already pointless,
the truth has gone to the bottom of
the most prosaic pit.
I have stifled too many things
to see them,
I have stifled the shine of a thing
believing it to be an ornament,
and when seduced
by the simplest things,
my love of depth
has hindered me.

EN LA PLAYA

Los caminantes
dejan líneas de pisadas,
cientos de líneas que se mezclan,
rivalizan,
y quien camina por la orilla solo
no puede despegar los ojos
de las huellas que lo precedieron.
Busca una afinidad,
un alma que se le parezca,
que no encuentra. Las huellas
le muestran cuán distinto es.
Todas, menos las suyas,
le parecen pulcras y lozanas.
Se siente defectuoso.
Olvida que no ve personas,
sino pies,
y ni siquiera pies, sino pisadas.

ON THE BEACH

The walkers
leave behind their footprints,
hundreds of tracks that get mixed up,
compete with one another,
and whoever walks the shore alone
cannot take his eyes
from the tracks that lie before him.
He seeks an affinity,
a soul resembling his own,
that he does not find. The tracks
show him how unique he is.
All of them, apart from his own,
seem neat and self-assured.
His own appear defective.
He forgets that he is not seeing people,
only feet,
and not even feet, but footprints.

HAY HERMANOS QUE NO APRENDEN

A mi hermano

Hay hermanos que no aprenden
con la edad a caminar parejos,
a nivelar sus años en la calle.
Uno se apura y se adelanta,
y el otro, pisando
el surco abierto por su hermano,
se ensimisma,
tomando el surco como propio,
aligerando la tarea del que abre paso,
de modo que el favor es mutuo:
el de adelante se hace cargo del trayecto
y deja al otro libre de soñar
y especular,
quizá de ver más lejos,
y el soñador, al emular
los pasos del hermano que se apura,
los absorbe
para que el otro sienta cada paso propio envuelto
en otros pasos que lo siguen,
que lo disculpan
y lo exoneran de pisar,
que borran cada paso suyo
para que vuele y no camine.

THERE ARE BROTHERS WHO DO NOT LEARN

To my brother

There are brothers who do not learn,
as they get older, to walk side by side,
to level out their years on the street.
One rushes ahead,
and the other, stepping into
the furrow opened by his brother,
retreats into himself,
making the furrow his own,
lightening the task of the one who has opened the way,
so that the favour is mutual:
the one who goes ahead takes charge of the journey
and leaves the other free to dream
and ponder,
perhaps to see further,
and the dreamer, by emulating
the steps of the brother who rushes ahead,
absorbs them,
so that the other feels his every step enveloped
by the footsteps that follow him,
that forgive him
and exonerate him,
that erase every step of his own
so that he doesn't walk but flies.

COMO DELANTE DE UN PRADO

Como delante de un prado una vaca
que inclina mansamente la cabeza
y sólo la levanta para contemplar su suerte,
o una ballena estacionada justo
en la corriente de una migración de plancton,
a veces me sorprendo estático
y hundido, estacionado
en medio del gran prado del lenguaje.
Pero no tengo dos estómagos
y hasta la vaca busca, cata, escoge,
separa cierta hierba que le gusta,
no es un edén el prado, es su trabajo,
y la ballena, cuando come el plancton,
separa las partículas más gruesas,
se gana el pan diario, su inmenso pan,
buscándolo en el fondo de los mares,
después emerge, expulsa el diablo de su cuerpo
y vuelve a sumergirse sin saber
si come el plancton o lo respira.
No es fácil ser cetáceo ni rumiante
y yo no tengo doble estómago y con uno
hay que escoger, no todo sirve,
sólo la poesía no desecha,
ve el mundo antes de comer.
Mundo en ayunas, ¿a qué sabes?
Poder hacer una única ingestión que dure de por vida,
que con un solo almuerzo nos alcance
y tener toda la vida para digerirlo...
Tener un grado de asimilación inmenso,

from *Delante de un prado una vaca (2011)*

AS BEFORE A MEADOW

As before a meadow a cow
placidly lowers her head
and only raises it to count her blessings,
or like a whale parked directly
in the path of migrating plankton,
sometimes I surprise myself, stalled
and overwhelmed, parked
amid the great meadow of language.
But I don't have two stomachs
and even the cow seeks out, samples, chooses,
singles out a particular grass that pleases her,
the meadow is not an Eden, it's her job,
and the whale, when he eats plankton,
filters out the coarser elements,
winning his daily bread, his immense bread,
seeking it out in the deeps of the sea,
later emerging to expel the devil from his body
and returning beneath the waves without knowing
whether he is eating plankton or breathing it.
It's not easy being a cetacean or a ruminant
and I don't have a double stomach, and even with one
I have to choose, not everything is suitable,
only poetry doesn't cast aside,
regards the world before eating.
Fasting world, how do you taste?
To be able to consume one single meal that lasts a lifetime,
that with a single meal we are sated
and have a lifetime to digest it . . .
to have an immense capacity for assimilation

saber que todo se digiere
y lo perdido da un rodeo y regresa.
Por eso escribo: para recobrar
del fondo todo lo adherido,
porque es el único rodeo en el que creo,
porque escribir abre un segundo estómago
en la especie.
El verso con su ácido remueve las partículas
dejadas por el plancton de los días
y a mí también, como el cetáceo,
me sale un chorro a veces,
una palabra vertical que rompe el tedio de los mares.

to know that everything's digested
and what is lost makes a detour and returns.
This is why I write: to recover
from the depths all that adheres there,
because it is the only detour in which I believe,
because to write opens a second stomach
in the species.
Verse with its acid removes the particles
left behind by the plankton of days
and from me also, like the cetacean,
a jet of water springs forth from time to time,
a vertical word that breaks the tedium of the seas.

QUERIDA EMILY

Querida Emily,
tu vida más pequeña que un pañuelo,
tu jardín, los dos lirios en la mano
con que abrías la puerta.

El reverendo, el juez,
la aldea de prados verdes
con su tedio,
y tu padre, la más dura de las puertas.

Sedienta de más vida y temerosa
de tenerla, ambigua siempre,
bajando la escalera cunado las visitas
habían tomado ya el camino de la puerta.

Sólo en tus versos, Emily,
bajaste a tiempo todos los peldaños
y no necesitaste flores para ir a abrir
la puerta.

Ni lirios, ni prados,
ni reverendos un jueces;
tú sola, en la miseria
de ese jardín humano, abriendo puertas.

DEAR EMILY

Dear Emily,
your life smaller than a handkerchief,
your garden, the two lilies in your hand
with which you opened the door.

The reverend, the judge,
the village with its green meadows,
with its tedium,
and your father, the most resilient of doors.

Thirsty for more life and fearful
of having it, always ambivalent,
going downstairs when the guests
had already made their way to the door.

Only in your verses, Emily,
did you descend all the steps in time
and you didn't need flowers to open
the door.

Neither lilies nor meadows,
neither reverends nor judges;
you alone, in the misery
of that human garden, opening doors.

OREJAS

Dos orejas: un para oír a los vivos
otra para oír a los muertos

las dos abiertas día y noche
las dos cerradas a nuestros sueños

para oír el silencio no te tapes las orejas
oirás la sangre que corre por tus venas

para oír el silencio aguza los oídos
escúchalo una vez y no vuelvas a oírlo

si te tapas la oreja izquierda oirás el infierno
si te tapas la derecha oirás . . . no te digo

había una tercera oreja pero no cabía en la cara
la ocultamos en el pecho y comenzó a latir

está rodeada de oscuridad
es la única oreja que el aire no engaña

es la oreja que nos salva de ser sordos
cuando allí arriba nos fallan las orejas

EARS

Two ears: one to hear the living
the other to hear the dead

both of them open night and day
both of them closed to our dreams

to hear silence don't cover the ears
you will hear the blood that runs through your veins

to hear silence prick up your ears
listen to it once and never hear it again

if you cover the left ear you will hear hell
if you cover the right you will hear . . . I'm not telling you

there was a third ear but it didn't fit on the face
we hid it in the chest and it began to throb

it is surrounded by darkness
and is the only ear the air does not deceive

it's the ear that saves us from deafness
when up above our ears fail us

MI HIJO JUEGA SOBRE MI LOMO

Todo padre es un caballo
    Antonio Deltoro

Mi hijo juega sobre mi lomo,
es un vaquero y lo llevo
a cuatro patas por la alfombra
espoleado por sus ¡arre caballo!,
pero sus pies ya tocan el piso,
no es el jinete de antes
que a horcajadas limpias se aferraba
a mi cuello, ahora percibe
su propio peso, deja de arrearme
y se baja. Me acuesto boca arriba,
él se acuesta también
y miramos el techo. Ya no soy
su caballo. No me lo dice,
pero lo piensa. Se bajó
para siempre de mí, su centauro,
a este suelo de todos
que da vuelta a la tierra.

MY SON PLAYS ON MY BACK

Every father is a horse
Antonio Deltoro

My son plays on my back,
he is a cowboy and I carry him
on all fours across the carpet
spurred on by his 'gee up horsey!'
but his feet now touch the ground,
he is not the jockey of yesteryear,
neatly astride me, who clung
to my neck; now he senses
his own weight, stops driving me on,
and dismounts. I lie on my back,
he lies down too
and we look at the ceiling. I am
no longer his horse. He doesn't say it,
but he thinks it. He has dismounted
from me, his centaur, forever,
onto the ground of all
that makes the world go around.

EL TAPETE PERSA

Tú no quieres que entre el sol en el cuarto
porque destiñe el tapete persa,

yo prefiero que entre el sol en el cuarto
aunque destiña el tapete persa.

Tapetes persas hay muchas te digo
y a los dos se nos acaban los días de sol.

Y tú: el sol entra en el cuarto una hora y se larga,
pero el tapete pesa relumbra todo el día

con todos sus colores.
Y yo: por eso el sol es el sol,

que entra en el cuarto y nos deslumbra
a cambio de llevarse unos colores,

pero un tapete persa descolorido,
no es un tapete sin colores,

relumbra del color de muchos días de sol
que sólo en los tapetes persas puede verse.

PERSIAN RUG

You don't want the sun coming into the bedroom
because it discolours the Persian rug,

I prefer the sun coming in to the bedroom
even though it discolours the Persian rug.

There are plenty of Persian rugs, I tell you,
and both of us are running out of sunny days.

And you: the sun enters the room one hour and departs,
but the Persian rug shines the whole day through

with all its colours.
And I: that's why the sun is the sun,

that comes into our bedroom and dazzles us
in exchange for taking away some colours,

but a discoloured Persian rug
is not a rug without colours,

it shines with the colour of many sunny days
that can only be seen in Persian rugs.

LOS PERROS LADRAN A LO LEJOS

Los perros ladran a lo lejos.
Junto con ellos soy
el único sin sueño en el planeta.
Me ladran a mí,
despiertos por mi culpa.
Mi estar despierto los encoleriza
y su cólera me espanta.
Somos los únicos
que no dudan
de la redondez de la tierra.
Los otros, los dormidos,
han renegado de Copérnico,
por esta única vez
se han reclinado sobre un mundo plano.
Por esta única vez, todas las noches,
y así amanecen,
creyendo que la tierra no da giros.
No pueden conciliar el sueño
sobre una superficie triste,
sobre un planeta equis.
Mejor oír ladrar los perros
que amanecer neolíticos.
Más vale no pegar el ojo
que claudicar del universo.

THE DOGS ARE BARKING IN THE DISTANCE

The dogs are barking in the distance.
Along with them I am
the only one on this planet who's not asleep.
They bark at me,
it's my fault they're awake.
My being awake angers them
and their anger scares me.
We are the only ones
who do not doubt
the roundness of the earth.
The others, those who are sleeping,
have disowned Copernicus,
for just this once
they have lain down on a flat world.
For just this once, every night,
and so they wake
believing that the earth doesn't turn.
They can't settle to sleep
on the sad surface
of a Planet X.
Better to hear the dogs bark
than wake to a neolithic dawn.
Better not to sleep a wink
than to give up on the universe.

TRES HORMIGAS

Tres hormigas en mi baño,
como todas las mañanas.

¿Serán las mismas o se turnan?

Tres exploradoras,
a ver si me ausento o me descuido

o despierto un poco más tarde,
que es lo que necesita el hormiguero
para cruzar el baño.

No me gusta matar hormigas,
sobre todo las conocidas
y, mientras cago,
muevo el pie para asustarlas.

Con eso espero que baste.

El hormiguero tendrá que esperar.

Condeno a una muchedumbre
a la inacción y a pasar hambre.
Se morirán muchísimas.

Pero, ¿qué puedo hacer?
En mi naturaleza está cuidar mi nido,
como ellas el suyo.

Sentado en el retrete, adormilado,
soy tan hormiga como todos,

alguien me observa de seguro
y ha decidido no pisarme.

THREE ANTS

Three ants in my bathroom,
just like every morning.

Are they the same or do they take turns?

Three explorers, checking whether
I'm absent or have dropped my guard

or have woken a little later,
giving the colony of ants
time to cross the bathroom.

I don't like killing ants,
especially ones I know,
and as I shit
I move my foot to scare them off.

So I hope that suffices.

The colony will have to wait.

I condemn a multitude
to idleness and starvation.
Many will die.

But what can I do?
It's in my nature to take care of my nest,
as they do theirs.

Sitting on the toilet, sleepy,
I'm as much an ant as anyone,

someone is watching me, for sure,
and has decided not to step on me.

MIRO EN LA TELEVISIÓN UN ELEFANTE HERIDO

Miro en la televisión un elefante
herido, rodeado de leones
que se lo están comiendo.
No hay en la tierra un animal
que pueda darle una muerte buena.
Corren suerte las gacelas, las cebras y los ñus:
el cuello quebrado, la asfixia
y el alivio. El elefante, en cambio,
es devorado vivo por la horda
que entre un bocado y otro
se trepa en él y otea la lejanía.
Les da lo mismo
que esa cosa enorme respire aún
y él, narcotizado por el miedo,
explica el locutor,
tal vez no sienta los mordiscos,
pero no estoy seguro.
Desmantelado a plena luz,
no hay nada que lo una a sus verdugos,
como sí une, entre nosotros, la tortura,
en que se lee el dolor del torturado
y se le acosa ahí, donde mas sufre.
Un dialogo bestial, perverso pero humano.
Aqui la pura extraccion de partes,
el vándalo saqueo,
la injuria de las vísceras que asoman,
perder sentido trozo a trozo,
perder la especie sin perder los ojos,
que son, conforme el resto es deglutido,
un ojo más y más ajeno al otro
y cada uno cada vez más puro,
casi un oasis de palmeras en el polvo.

ON THE TELEVISION I WATCH A WOUNDED ELEPHANT

On the television I watch a wounded
elephant, surrounded by lions
that are consuming him.
There is no creature on earth
that could give him a good death.
Gazelles, zebras and wildebeests are lucky:
the broken neck, suffocation
and relief. The elephant, by contrast,
is devoured alive by the pride
that between one bite and the next
clamber over him and gaze into the distance.
It is a matter of indifference to them
that this enormous thing still breathes
and he, drugged by fear,
as the voiceover explains,
perhaps does not feel the bites,
but I am not so sure.
Dismantled in broad daylight,
nothing binds him to his executioners,
such as, between us humans, torture might,
in which the pain of the tortured can be read
and he is thus tormented, suffering most terribly.
A bestial dialogue, perverse but human.
Instead, we have the simple extraction of body parts,
the plundering vandal,
the insult to his exposed guts,
losing consciousness piece by piece,
losing the species without losing the eyes,
which are, like the rest of him, swallowed,
one eye ever more distant from the other
and each one ever purer,
almost an oasis of palm trees in the dust.

A cada cual su cielo (2021)

ESCRIBO PROSA MIENTRAS JUNTO VALOR

Escribo prosa mientras junto
valor para los versos,
escribo prosa para que los versos
se escriban casi solos,
escribo prosa como quien empuja
un buey por un cultivo.

Cuánta prosa para juntar
valor para los versos,
cuántas palabras con esfuerzo
llevadas al final de cada línea,
cuántos renglones rectos
por no saber salir del surco.

from *A cada cual su cielo* (2021)

I WRITE PROSE WHILE GATHERING COURAGE

I write prose while gathering
courage to write verse,
I write prose so that the poems
can almost write themselves,
I write prose like one who drives
an ox to plough a field.

All that prose to gather
courage for the poems,
all those words dragged by force
to the end of every phrase,
all those straight lines
because I didn't know how to leave the furrow.

HAY ÁRBOLES QUE NACEN PARA BOSQUE

Hay árboles que nacen para bosque
y otros que son un bosque sin saberlo.
El árbol ignora el bosque
y el bosque tal vez ignora el árbol,
lo único que sabemos es la raíz que escarba
y la rama que también escarba,
una en su cielo de barro,
la otra en su cielo de nube.
La vida es escarbar y a cada cual su cielo.

THERE ARE TREES THAT ARE BORN FOR THE FOREST

There are trees that are born for the forest
and others that are a forest without knowing it.
The tree ignores the forest
and perhaps the forest ignores the tree,
all we know is the root that rummages
and the branch that also rummages,
one in its sky of mud,
the other in its sky of cloud.
Life is rummaging, and to each of us our sky.

NO IDENTIFICADA

En la orilla del grupo,
casi fuera de cuadro, está él,
la persona no identificada,
como asienta la nota de pie.
No es famoso,
tal vez se coló en el banquete.
Reaparece un poco más visible
en otra foto, en otro sitio,
con otro grupo de ilustres.
La nota al pie refrenda:
persona no identificada.
En la última foto
volvemos a encontrarlo,
ahora en el centro de los otros retratados,
a los que abraza sonriendo,
y ellos sonríen y lo abrazon a su vez,
todos con nombre y apellido menos él,
que no fue identificado.

UNIDENTIFIED

You find him on the edge of the group,
almost out of the picture,
the unidentified person,
as the footnote attests.
He's not famous,
maybe he gategrashed the dinner.
He appears a little more visibly
in another photo, in another place
with another group of the great and the good,
The footnote affirms:
unidentified.
In the last photo
we find him once again,
this time in the middle of the group portrait,
embracing the others,
and they are all smiling and embracing him in turn,
all with a first and last name except for him,
who was not identified.

PARA LLEGAR A PUEBLA

¡Tantos años sin saber ir a Puebla,
a qué altura de qué arteria hay que salir
para llegar a Puebla,
que está a dos horas!
La gente va a Puebla y regresa
el mismo día,
yo mismo he estado en Puebla
(¿quién no ha estado en Puebla?),
¡y tantos años sin saber cómo ir!

Enséñenme a ir a Puebla,
que está a dos horas,
y a creer en Dios,
que está tan cerca, que se llega a Dios
y se regresa de Dios el mismo día.
Yo mismo he creído en Dios
(¿quién no ha creído en Dios?).
Me pasa con Él lo mismo que con Puebla,
no sé a qué altura de qué arteria hay que salir.

¿Qué ha sido de mi vida
si no he aprendido lo que todos saben:
hablarle a Dios e ir y volver de Puebla el mismo día?
Yo solo sé el camino a Cuernavaca,
es todo lo que sé para salir de esta ciudad.

Enséñenme el camino a Puebla,
enséñenme a salir, a creer, a ir
y regresar el mismo día.

TO GET TO PUEBLA

So many years without knowing how to get to Puebla,
which junction of which artery you have to take
to get to Puebla,
only two hours distant!
People go to Puebla and return
the same day,
I myself have been to Puebla
(who hasn't been to Puebla?)
and so many years without knowing how to get there!

Show me how to get to Puebla,
which is two hours distant,
and to believe in God,
who is so close that He can be reached
and returned from the same day.
I myself have believed in God
(who hasn't believed in God?)
The same thing happens with Him as with Puebla,
I don't know which junction of which artery to take.

What has become of my life
that I haven't learned what everyone knows:
to speak with God and to visit and return from Puebla the
same day?
I only know the road to Cuernavaca,
that's the only way I know to leave this city.

Show me the road to Puebla,
show me how to leave, to believe, to go
and return the same day.

SUBÍ A COLGAR LAS SÁBANAS

Subí a colgar las sábanas,
en la azotea estaba el cielo
y abajo me esperaba un libro.

Tenía prisa de volver,
pero se me abrió el cielo
como una página
y me olvidé del libro.

Me viene del cielo,
no de los libros, la certeza
de que el cielo es solo cielo.

Me seca de todo residuo de Dios,
como el sol y el viento
secan las sábanas.

Miro cómo en ellas lo húmedo
se retira
y, secas ya, libre de Dios, se agitan.

I WENT TO HANG SOME SHEETS

I went up to hang some sheets,
and above the roof terrace was the sky
and below a book awaited me.

I was in a hurry to return,
but the sky opened up to me
like a page
and I forgot the book.

The certainty that the sky
is only sky comes to me not from
books, but from the sky itself.

Just as the sun and wind
dry the sheet, the sky wrings from me
all residue of God.

I watch how the dampness in the sheets
vanishes and, dry now,
free of God, they flutter.

ME GUSTARÍA PARA ESPERARTE

Me gustaría para esperarte
sacar una silla a la calle,
pero ya nadie saca sillas a la calle.
Había en mi casa una silla
que se destinaba a eso,
guardaba un lugar aparte,
ninguna salía excepto ella.
La silla de la calle.

AS I WAIT FOR YOU

As I wait for you, I would like
to put a chair out on the street,
but nowadays no one puts
chairs out on the street.
There was a chair in my house
whose purpose was just that,
it was kept in a place apart,
no other chair went out except for it.
The chair for putting on the street.

¿Qué ha sido de las guitarras
en las esquinas,
en los paraderos de camiones,
en las estaciones del metro
o afuera de una iglesia?
La calle era pródiga en guitarras,
que algunos tocaban por dinero
y otros por ser jóvenes.
Se encontraban las guitarras
en sentido contrario,
se detenían durante unos acordes
y luego proseguía cada guitarra su canción
y su camino.
Había ventanas. Había mujeres
en las ventanas que se asomaban
a buscar la primera guitarra del día,
que retribuían con monedas o con un beso.
¡Cuántas ventanas al acecho de guitarras,
cuántos arpegios por lo bajo
anunciando una guitarra que venía
y cuántas mujeres sin celular en la mano!
Cuántos besos por simplemente saber tocar
la guitarra y cuántos hijos
nacidos de parejas que unió
una guitarra. Cuántas playas.
Cuántas playas con su hoguera
alrededor de una guitarra
y cómo al cambiar de mano su madera
lanzaba un destello de fuego.

WHAT HAS BECOME OF THE GUITARS?

What has become of the guitars
on street corners,
in lorry parks,
in metro stations
or outside churches?
The street was once rife with guitars,
that some played for money
and others because they were young.
You met the guitars
coming from the opposite direction,
they hung about for a few chords
and each guitar would proceed with its song
and on its way.
There were windows. There were women
at the windows, leaning out
looking for the first guitar of the day,
who would pay with coins or with a kiss.
So many windows spying on guitars,
so many arpeggios down below
announcing a guitar was on its way
and so many women without cell phones in their hands!
So many kisses for simply knowing how to play
the guitar and so many children
born to couples that a guitar
brought together. So many beaches.
So many beaches with a campfire
around a guitar
how at the stroke of a hand its wood
set off a flash of fire.

Cuántas guitarras casi mudas
se veían en los camiones
donde las tocaban viejos de voz ronca.
Santo el que inventó la guitarra
y santo el que inventó la limosna,
pero más santo el que inventó los besos.

So many almost mute guitars
to be seen in trucks
where old men played, singing with a raspy voice.
Blessed the one who invented the guitar
and blessed whoever invented alms,
but more blessed still the one who invented kisses.

TODA LA NOCHE EN VELA

Toda la noche en vela,
oyendo unos ladridos
que vienen de quién sabe dónde.

Toda la noche en blanco
para que otros crucen
incólumes la noche.

Para que duerman
los de párpados más finos
estamos nosotros, los sin párpados,

con nuestra lámpara
prendida,
ignorados, ignorándonos.

Por esas lámparas
se apagan las jaurías
que solo oímos los insomnes.

ALL NIGHT SLEEPLESS

All night sleepless,
listening to that barking
from who knows where.

All night wide awake
so that others might cross
the night unscathed.

So that those with finer eyelids
might sleep, that's why we're here,
we with no eyelids,

with our lamp
turned on,
ignored, ignoring ourselves.

By those lamps are silenced
the packs of dogs
that only insomniacs can hear.

¿Y SI YA NO DIERA DE SÍ LA FRUTA?

¿Y si ya no diera de sí la fruta?
¿Si dejara de colgar de los árboles
y de madurar en el suelo?
¿Si ya no hubiera cítricos,
ni siquiera nueces?
¿Qué sería de nuestros brazos,
de nuestros célebres pulgares,
nacidos para arrancarla?
Todas las distancias
nacieron de la fruta,
que debimos recoger
en la rama de al lado,
en el árbol de junto,
en el bosque contiguo,
en la tribu al otro lado del río.
Nos impulsó la fruta,
nos dispersó desde el principio.
Detrás de cada lujo,
de cada anhelo,
de cada viaje, su dulzura.
La carne misma la comemos
como fruta y no como carne,
la arrancamos de un rebaño de carne
como se arranca la fruta más madura,
todo lo suculento cae a nuestra boca
como descolgado de una rama,
como tú, que arranco cada día
de tu árbol, de tu tribu
y te traigo a este lado del río
y te como y te muerdo y te guardo
y tengo miedo que te pudras.

AND IF THE FRUIT NO LONGER GAVE ITSELF?

And if the fruit no longer gave itself?
If it stopped hanging from the trees
and ripening on the ground?
If there were no more citrus
or even nuts?
What would become of our arms,
of our famous thumbs,
born to pluck?
All distances
were born from the fruit
that we must pick
on the next branch,
on the nearby tree,
in the adjoining forest,
in the tribe across the river.
Fruit drove us onward,
scattered us from the start.
Behind every luxury,
every desire,
every journey – its sweetness.
Meat too we eat like fruit
and not like meat,
we pluck it from a flock of meat
as the ripest fruit is plucked
all that is succulent
falls into our mouths
as if shaken from a branch,
like you, who I pluck every day
from your tree, from your tribe
and bring you to this side of the river
and eat you and bite you and keep you
and fear that you will rot.

EN LA ANTÁRTIDA

En la Antártida
no prosperó la pelambre.

Ahí nunca llegaron el oso,
el lobo, el buey almizclero.

Se resguardó el latido
bajo una gran capa de grasa,

la grasa que redondea las formas,
y las formas redondas prefieren el agua.

Qué mal se mueven en el suelo
el pingüino y la morsa.

Cuánta torpeza en la Antártida,
cuántas maromas de circo.

La Antártida y la grasa de sus focas.
La Antártida y las plumas de sus aves.

No ha prosperado la pelambre
y en el aire viajan libres,

sin el estorbo de árboles y frutos,
los olores que azuzan el hambre.

Nada se oculta en la Antártida,
no hay acechos, solo distancias,

IN ANTARCTICA

In Antarctica
pelts do not flourish.

The bear never came here,
nor the wolf, the musk ox.

The heartbeat was protected
beneath a heavy layer of fat,

the fat that surrounds forms,
and round forms prefer water.

How ungainly their movements on the ground,
the penguin and the walrus.

So much clumsiness in Antarctica,
so many circus somersaults.

Antarctica and the fat of its seals,
Antarctica and the plumage of its birds.

The pelt has not prospered
and in the air flight is free,

without the hindrance of trees and fruits,
the smells that stir the appetite.

Nothing is hidden in Antarctica,
there is no lying in wait, only distance,

se sale a cazar en manada,
se huye en rebaño y cardumen,

se vive y se muere apretados
y la agonía se desconoce.

En invierno, antes que el mar se congele,
la grasa abandona la Antártida.

Solo queda el pingüino,
que emprende su marcha

alejándose del mar,
y por única vez

una línea increíble de huellas
atraviesa la losa de hielo.

Y por única vez, donde todo se borra,
queda un surco, un anhelo visible

que hace que la Antártida
emerja por completo.

they hunt in packs,
they flee in herd and shoal,

they live and die crowded close
and agony is unknown.

In winter, before the sea freezes,
fat abandons Antarctica.

Only the penguin remains,
setting out on his march

moving far from the sea,
and for once only

an incredible line of tracks
crosses the slab of ice.

And for once only, where everything is erased,
there remains a furrow, a visible longing

that allows Antarctica
to fully emerge.

SOY LA ÚLTIMA PERSONA

Soy la última persona,
el último hablante de un idioma, el mío,
que pende enteramente de mi lengua,
todo un acervo de palabras
que va a caer en el olvido
el día que me despida de mi aliento,
mi lengua que hablo a solas y que olvido
porque dejó de ser idioma y es solo acervo.
Muchas de sus palabras ya están muertas
porque no volveré a decirlas,
y aunque las diga, todo lo que diga,
por no tener a nadie que me entienda,
es un invento mío, pese a que se parezca
en todo a las palabras que aprendí de niño,
y a veces me pregunto si no somos todos
los últimos hablantes de lo que decimos.

I AM THE LAST PERSON

I am the last person,
the last speaker of a language, my own,
that hangs entirely on my tongue,
a whole heritage of words
that will fall into oblivion
the day I breathe my last,
the language that I speak to myself and that I forget
because it has ceased to be a language and is only a heritage.
Many of its words are already dead
because I will not utter them again,
and even if I say them, everything that I say,
for lack of anyone who understands me,
is my own invention, despite my words resembling
in every detail the words I learned as a child,
and sometimes I wonder if we are not all
the last speakers of the things we say.

MIENTRAS ME HABLAS

Mientras me hablas
de lo mal que está todo,
te olvidas de tu sopa,
dejas la cuchara en el plato
y agitas las manos.
Te escucho con atención
mientras miro de reojo tu sopa que se enfría.
Terminé la mía hace cinco minutos
y no te has dado cuenta.
Dices que todo está mal
y se está fomrando una pátina fea
en la superficie de tu sopa,
que dentro de poco será un coágulo incomible.
Coge tu cuchara y come,
no agregues más tristeza a todo con otra sopa fría.

WHILE YOU SPEAK TO ME

While you speak to me
of all that is wrong with the world,
you forget your soup,
you leave your spoon in the bowl
and wave your hands about.
I listen attentively
as I watch, from the corner of my eye,
your soup getting cold.
I finished mine five minutes ago
and you haven't noticed.
You say that everything is wrong
and an ugly skin is forming
on the surface of your soup,
that soon will be an inedible paste.
Pick up your spoon and eat,
don't add more sadness to it all with cold soup.

EL HOMICIDIO NO ES LO MÍO

El homicidio no es lo mío.
Ningún humano, por lo pronto.
Quizá un insecto, algún mosquito
que aplasté con una chancla contra el muro.
Un crimen deleznable.
Algo bien equipado de órganos
e instinto,
de decisiones bien o mal tomadas,
ya no se mueve por mi culpa.
Ahí está la mancha en la pared,
la vida aniquilada de un chanclazo,
sin ni siquiera una declaración
de guerra previa. Su vida
era tan vida como la que más.
Lo diminuto late igual o más que el resto.
Tomemos la lombriz. Creemos que se arrastra,
y en cambio avanza
usando limpiamente sus apéndices,
erguida de una forma incomprensible para todo aquel
que no camina como los anélidos.
Nada se arrastra en la naturaleza,
la vida esté de pie o ya no es vida.
Por eso, cuando mueres,
mueres como un mosquito: de un chanclazo.
No hay otra forma de dejar de ser.
Ahí estás, manchando un muro,
aunque desfilen multitudes en tu entierro.
Respeta pues a todo aquel que estrujas
contra la pared,
mira sin asco sus vísceras que escurren;
si bien lo ves, la suciedad casi no existe,

MURDER IS NOT MY THING

Murder is not my thing.
Not of a human, at least for now.
Perhaps an insect, some mosquito
that I squashed with a sandal against the wall.
An abhorrent crime.
Something well equipped with organs
and instinct,
with decisions well or badly taken,
no longer moves because of me.
There is the stain on the wall,
the life rubbed out by a flip-flop,
without even a prior
declaration of war. Its life
as much a life as any other,
its tiny heartbeat the same or greater than the rest.
Let us consider the worm. We believe that it crawls,
and instead it advances
using its appendages dextrously,
upright in a way incomprehensible to anyone
who does not walk like an annelid.
Nothing crawls in nature,
life is upright or is no longer life.
That's why, when you die,
you die like a mosquito: with a blow from a flip-flop.
There's no other way of ceasing to be.
There you are, staining a wall,
though crowds might turn out for your funeral.
So respect everything you crush
against the wall,
look without disgust at the viscera that drain away;
although you see it, the dirt is almost non-existent,

hay solo cosas fuera de lugar,
cosas salidas de contexto,
y a eso lo llamamos excremento,
cuando las cosas, es bien sabido,
se salen de contexto todo el tiempo
y el excremento es algo intrínseco y vital.
Es sucio solo el cuerpo que torturan,
tratado todo él como excremento,
sin corporalidad y sin contexto,
como se tira aquello que no sirve.
El fuego conmemora,
consume, o sea recuerda, y nada humano
se acerca a su pericia.
La diferencia entre cenizas y basura.

there are only things out of place,
things out of context,
and which we call excrement,
whereas things, as is well known,
go out of context all the time
and excrement is something vital and intrinsic.
Only the tortured body is dirty,
treated as though it were excrement,
without corporality and without context,
just as what is useless is thrown away.
Fire commemorates,
consumes – in other words, remembers –
and nothing human comes close in expertise.
The difference between ashes and garbage.

WRITING IN ANOTHER MOTHER TONGUE

I first stepped inside Fabio Morábito's world in May 2014, when I attended a writers' group (*tertulia*) that he has led for many years, in the upstairs space of a large cafeteria in Mexico City. I had been taken there by two friends, the poets Pedro Serrano and Carlos López Beltrán. Towards the end of the meeting, I was asked to read the Spanish versions of some of my own poems and can recall being shrouded in a miasma of imposter syndrome. As a non-Mexican, reading my work to a group of hospitable but inquisitive Mexican poets – attentive, I could sense, to every nuance of my spoken Spanish – the net effect was to bring on a self-questioning that had recurred a few times already in that vast, sprawling city: *what on earth am I doing here?*

I need not have concerned myself. Being a foreigner, and an outsider to the Spanish language, is one with which Morábito is himself familiar. The son of Italians, Fabio was born in Alexandria, Egypt, but spent much of his childhood in Milan before migrating to Mexico with his family at the age of fifteen, and learning Spanish as a second language. He had already, by then, acquired all the characteristics of the budding literary nomad.

The opening lines of one of his best-known poems sets out the core of the matter. In my translation, the poem begins: 'Because I write in a language / that I learned, / I have to be awake / while others sleep… I write before daybreak, / when I am almost the only one awake, / and can make mistakes / in a language that I learned.'

'To those who inquire,' writes Morábito, in a short essay revealingly titled 'Writing in Someone Else's House'[1], 'I always have the answer that, with regard to Spanish, I have the sensation of having caught the last train, and I add that the train had already started moving, and I had to run so as not to miss it.' 'Perhaps I'm wrong', he continues, 'and the train did in fact leave without me. It is a doubt I can't stop thinking about and perhaps the one that underlies much or all of what I write.'

In the same article, Morábito claims that after including this poem in his collection *Alguien de Lava* (2002) his publisher called him to question the accuracy of the phrase 'in a language that I learned'. All languages are learned, the publisher told him, including one's own. This remark provoked Morábito into a debate with himself about the different ways by which we acquire our mother tongue and any languages that might follow: while it is incontestable that we all 'learn' our mother tongue, we do not learn it in the same way that we subsequently learn other languages. Such is the extent of Morábito's preoccupation with his own linguistic formation that three of the poems included in this selection, written at different stages in the poet's career, address, respectively, his complex and sometimes precarious relationship with Spanish ('Because I write'); the apparent desertion of (or his fear of losing) his Italian ('Now, after almost twenty years'); and a sort of threnody ('I am the last person'), which worries at the thought that the Italian that the poet continues to speak to himself in middle age 'has ceased to be a language and is only a heritage'.

In the second of these poems, the poet considers how the language of his childhood now 'slips through his hands', 'becomes cold' and 'breaks away in fragments'. Perplexed, he wonders 'With what words / will I recall my childhood, / with what will I reconstruct / the way and its wonders? / How will I complete the circle of my years?' And that final question, which in Spanish reads '¿Cómo completaré mi edad?' – caused me to undergo one of those translation crises with which all of us translators are familiar. The phrase literally means: 'how will I complete my age', and after lengthy consultations with the poet and a fellow translator, I arrived at the formulation in the text, but not without some misgivings, and not without the poet having to explain to me, in granular detail, the exact texture and resonance that the phrase held for him. Although I frequently communicate with the poets I translate, it is sometimes the case that they have a command of English: not so with Fabio, which led to an even more interesting than usual discussion about the temperature or microclimate generated by particular words or phrases in Spanish. I wonder whether I would have had such a probing conversation with a poet who had never written in anything but his native tongue. It is a question Fabio raises in the essay already cited, when he claims that 'no one like the writer who comes from another language is as sensitive to the voracious and demanding nature of writing. Experiencing in the first person writing's ability to disfigure a lived experience, reinventing it from the root, their awareness of style will be in principle much sharper than that of the native writer.' For the parvenu writer, he tells us, 'style is everything.' This immediately raises questions about the concern with style shown by other writers who wrote in their second (or third) languages, such as Conrad, Beckett, and perhaps most vividly, given his extraordinary devotion to style, Nabokov.

The quality of my exchanges with Fabio, and the conclusions we, or rather I, reached – as Fabio always deferred to me as translator – were informed by Fabio's own expertise as a translator from Italian to Spanish (including the work of such eminent poets as Ungaretti, Pavese and Montale). Unlike most of us, Fabio translates from his mother tongue into a language which, he says, 'is not my mother tongue but which I would like to believe has become my mother tongue'. He became a translator into Spanish as a way of building confidence, and with time the balance shifted, Spanish replacing Italian as his stronger language.

The question of language leads naturally enough to that of Morábito's Mexicanness (*mexicanidad*). On the same visit to Mexico City that I met Fabio, I spent some time with the translator Lucrecia Orensanz, who had put into Spanish a talk that I was due to deliver about Welsh poetry, in commemoration of the Dylan Thomas centenary, and during the course of a long bus journey across the city, Lucrecia explained to me what she believed *mexicanidad* amounted to. She suggested that Mexican culture is difficult for the outsider to penetrate, lacks porosity, resists integration. Lucrecia's own family had left Argentina after the military coup in 1976, when she was a small child, the family settling in Baja California, where her father worked as a marine biologist. Lucrecia said that although she had been in Mexico since the age of five, and spoke Spanish like a Mexican, there was an identifiable something about her, a 'foreigner' quality that Mexicans noticed and which consequently made her feel like one. Mexicans, she told me, are keenly aware of their *mexicanidad* and are quick to recognise it (or its absence) among themselves and others.

After the tertulia with Fabio's writing group, I walked with Pedro and Carlos through Mixcoac, the barrio in which Octavio Paz, Mexico's only Nobel laureate, spent his childhood. Paz regularly reminds his readers that for the Mexican, the pre-Columbian past is always a presence. The conquistadores might have razed Tenochtitlán to build Mexico City, but they could not wipe it from the face of the earth, even if they built over its remains. In his Nobel Prize Speech, Paz noted: 'The temples and gods of pre-Columbian Mexico are a pile of ruins, but the spirit that breathed life into that world has not disappeared; it speaks to us in the hermetic language of myth, legend, forms of social coexistence, popular art, customs. Being a Mexican writer means listening to the voice of that present, that presence.'[2] So it is that, despite all attempts to destroy it, Tenochtitlán has survived, reinventing itself along the way, and contributing to that often fraught synthesis of the indigenous and the colonial that still defines Mexican culture today.

Within such a structure, Fabio might be considered an outsider, and yet he remains one of Mexico's most acclaimed and best-loved poets. How to account for this apparent contradiction? In a lucid appraisal of the poet, titled 'The Stateless Verse of Fabio Morábito' the Spanish poet and critic Francisco José Cruz writes of Fabio's 'unrepentantly nomadic condition... the feeling of not entirely belonging anywhere' which 'develops within him a razor-sharp consciousness of provisionality;' that his is the 'poetry of a loner who seeks to pass by unperceived'.[3] I believe that it is precisely because of the facility with which he describes these nomadic tendencies that Fabio's work is so accessible; he describes his foreignness, his outsider status, in a way that is familiar to all of us, is part of the universal experience. He achieves this, at least in part, because writers – most especially poets – are forever reaching out beyond language in order to express the ineffable (that 'other tiger' that lies beyond the poem, as Borges would have it), and they are more susceptible than most to a state of linguistic anxiety. Discussing his own relationship to Spanish, and of his desire for 'total identification' with that language, he writes: 'I wonder if a dilemma like this is not something inherent to all who write; I wonder, therefore, if we who write are not all native speakers of another language and we write to cauterise a wound that separates us from the language and, thus, to feel again as if a language were our mother tongue, and a reality, which at some moment were revealed to us as foreign.'[4]

To conclude, I would like to mention a poem that, for me, exemplifies Morábito's achievement, offering snapshots from the other side of the mirror. 'Journey to Patzcuaro', which chronicles an adventure undertaken by the sixteen-year-old Fabio, only a year after his arrival in Mexico, was one of the poems I most enjoyed in this collection. There is a special delight in accomplishing a translation of a poem in one clean sweep that is at once similar to, but different from, the sense of achievement in one's 'own' work. Fabio speaks of this in an interview with Barbara Bertoni, when he says that to translate a poem that you love is 'to chew it over, appropriate it almost organically… rewriting that which was already written. It is a way of understanding something that cannot be fully understood by a simple reading, by trying to pin down what you feel might otherwise flee.' [5] In 'Journey to Pátzcuaro', arriving in the town at dawn, the young poet crosses the empty plaza, the sun's first rays illuminating a statue; he observes the deserted doorways, and no one can hear him, no one see him, 'like in a painting by De Chirico.' In an extraordinarily lucid moment, the adult poet reflects on his decision to reject the offer of a fine room, spacious and well-lit, overlooking the square and its statue, because he 'didn't dare take it', a decision, he says, that, had he chosen differently, might have changed his life forever: 'Maybe now I would be someone else, / everything would be different, / I wouldn't write what I write.' This recreation of the fragility of the fleeting moment, in an unfamiliar town in a new country, strikes me as encapsulating much else that we learn from Morábito's poetry, as though we too were setting out in a strange land, confronted by an array of decisions to be made, any one of which might mark us for eternity. It is this exposure to the unknown that venturing into the work of a new poet will sometimes afford us, and whose elusive texture I can only hope is transmitted by these translations also.

ENDNOTES:

1. 'Writing in Someone Else's House' in *Latin American Literature Today*, Issue 14, May 2020, translated by Lawrence Schimel.
2. Octavio Paz, Nobel Lecture, December 8, 1990.
3. Francisco José Cruz, 'The Stateless Verse of Fabio Morábito', in *Latin American Literature Today*, Issue 14, May 2020, translated by Arthur Malcolm Dixon.
4. 'Writing in Someone Else's House' ibid.
5. Barbara Bertoni, 'El músculo del traductor: una conversación con Fabio Morábito', *Periódico de Poesía*, 26 August, 2019 (my translation).